CELEBRITY SECRETS

REALITY TV STARS

ADAM SUTHERLAND

WAYLAND

First published in 2012 by Wayland

Copyright © Wayland 2012

Wayland
338 Euston Road
London NW1 3BH

Wayland Australia
Level 17/207 Kent Street
Sydney, NSW 2000

Editor: Nicola Edwards
Designer: Emil Dacanay
Picture Researcher: Shelley Noronha

Picture Acknowledgements: The author and publisher would like to thank the following for allowing their pictures to be reproduced in this publication:
Cover: Joe Seer / Shutterstock.com; p1 Featureflash / Shutterstock.com; p2 Featureflash / Shutterstock.com; p4 Joe Seer / Shutterstock.com; p5 Kevan Brooks/ AdMedia / Shutterstock.com; p6 Leon Neal/AFP/Getty Images; Dave J Hogan/ Getty Images; p8 Steve Vas / Featureflash / Shutterstock.com; p9 Eamonn McCormack/ Redferns/ Getty Images; p10 WireImage; p11 Helga Esteb / Shutterstock.com; p12 Featureflash / Shutterstock.com; p13 Dave Hogan/Getty Images; p14 Helga Esteb / Shutterstock.com; p15 Joe Seer / Shutterstock.com; p16 Featureflash / Shutterstock.com; p17 Ferdaus Shamim / WireImage; p18 Helga Esteb / Shutterstock. com; p19 Featureflash / Shutterstock.com; p20 Helga Esteb / Shutterstock.com; p21 Karl Mondon/MCT/MCT via Getty Images; p22 (t) Featureflash / Shutterstock.com, (m) Featureflash / Shutterstock.com, (b) Joe Seer / Shutterstock.com; p23 (t) Helga Esteb / Shutterstock.com, (m) Featureflash / Shutterstock.com, (b) Helga Esteb / Shutterstock.com; p24 Shutterstock.com/ © Pitroviz

British Library Cataloguing in Publication Data

Sutherland, Adam.
 TV reality stars. – (Celebrity secrets)
 1. Television personalities–Biography–Juvenile literature. 2. Reality television programs–Juvenile literature.
 I. Title II. Series
 791.4'5'0922-dc23

 ISBN: 978 0 7502 6776 2

Printed in China

Wayland is a division of Hachette Children's Books, an Hachette UK company

www.hachette.co.uk

Contents

Kim Kardashian

THE QUEEN OF REALITY TV

Kim's friends used to tell her that her family would be perfect for a reality show. Now 'Kardashian' is one of the best-known names on television!

Kim's name is on the list of the people with the most Twitter followers in the world — along with Lady Gaga, Justin Bieber, Barack Obama and Britney Spears.

Stats!

Name: Kimberley Noel Kardashian

Date and place of birth: 21 October 1980 in Los Angeles, California, USA

Education: Kim attended the all-girl Marymount High School in Beverly Hills, where she was friends with Paris Hilton.

Big break: Kim's mum (and manager) Kris Jenner persuaded the US entertainment channel E! to make a documentary about her family. The show, *Keeping Up With The Kardashians*, following the lives of Kim, older sister Kourtney and younger sister Khloé, has been a huge hit.

Major achievements: Kim has built a business empire based on her reality TV success. She has launched a chain of clothing stores with her sisters, and promotes perfume, jewellery, shoes, make-up and dozens of other products.

Additional TV appearances: In 2011 Kim starred with one of her sisters in *Kourtney And Kim Take New York*, which followed them opening a new clothing store in the city. Kim has also appeared on *Dancing With The Stars*, drama series *90210*, and was a guest judge on *America's Next Top Model*.

Secrets of success: Kim is a brilliant networker (with 8 million Twitter followers), who has used her on-screen popularity to become a very successful brand.

Life Story

For a girl who grew up in a Beverly Hills mansion with a swimming pool in the garden, Kim Kardashian is not afraid of hard work. Kim's father, who died in 2003, was a successful LA lawyer whose grandparents emigrated from Armenia in the 19th century. Kim has often stated how important her Armenian background is to her. Despite the family's wealth, Kim's father taught his daughters to stand on their own two feet and earn their own money.

Kim with sisters Khloé (far left) and Kourtney (centre) at the launch of the Kardashian Collection in LA, in 2011.

When fame came calling on Kim with the success of E! channel's *Keeping Up With The Kardashians*, she realised that for every downside — the loss of privacy, the pressure of living your life in front of TV cameras — there was an upside. People were interested in what you wore, where you shopped, what you ate, and how you stayed fit and healthy. So Kim started providing her fans with updates on her life.

Before long, Kim had launched her own range of best-selling fragrances, published an autobiography *Kardashian Konfidential*, and become the executive producer of a reality show called *The Spin Crowd*, about a friend's public relations firm. Kim is now estimated to be the highest earning reality star in the world.

Questions and Answers

Q Is everything in *Keeping Up With The Kardashians* real?

A 'People come up and tell me all the time that our show is like the perfectly written sitcom – but it's real! Everything we do and what we go through, that's what's really happening.'

Kim Kardashian, *The Times* 2011

Q Has social networking helped you become closer to your fans?

A '[Absolutely.] Whatever was printed [in the papers] used to be the last word. But it's not like that any more. I can get on Twitter and have a say too, if I feel like it.'

Kim Kardashian, *The Times* 2011

Ashley Banjo

DANCING ROLE MODEL

Ashley talks to the press after Diversity's surprise victory in the 2009 final of 'Britain's Got Talent'.

Diversity's success has meant that Ashley has had to put his degree on hold. He intends to finish it one day and become a forensic scientist!

Stats!

Name: Ashley Banjo

Date and place of birth: 4 October 1988 in Leytonstone, London, UK

Education: Ashley took four A-levels at Seevic College in Thundersley, Essex, achieving two A grades and two Bs. He went on to Queen Mary College in London to study Natural Sciences.

Big break: The son of a boxer and a professional ballerina, Ashley formed the dance troupe Diversity with his brother Jordan and nine friends. In 2009, with Ashley choreographing all the routines, they entered — and won — the ITV show *Britain's Got Talent*, beating the singer Susan Boyle in a final that was watched by 19 million people!

Major achievements: Thanks to their *Britain's Got Talent* victory, Diversity performed in front of the Queen at the 2009 Royal Variety Show, and at the Pride of Britain Awards. Tickets for their 2010 nationwide tour sold out in less than 24 hours.

Additional TV appearances: Ashley has been a judge on all three series of the TV talent show *Got To Dance* and hosts his own series *Ashley Banjo's Secret Street Crew* on Sky One.

Secrets of success: Hard work, dedication and focus have helped Ashley reach the top of his profession. A three-minute dance routine can take three months to choreograph and perfect.

Life Story

Ashley Banjo is one of Britain's best-known dancers. The Diversity choreographer and group spokesman grew up around his parents' dance school in Essex, and credits dancing — and his parents' guidance — for giving him a sense of purpose and the desire to achieve something with his life.

Questions and Answers

Q How important is dancing to you?

'Dancing has always been an escape to me. It was a way to stay off the streets. If I've learnt anything from dancing, it's that if you have a talent, you should never give it up.'

Ashley Banjo, *Love It* 2010

Q Would you recommend people entering TV talent shows?

'[Absolutely] *Britain's Got Talent* doesn't claim to turn you into a star, but it gives you a platform to perform. For us, it's changed our lives... Two years ago I was just an average person on the street with a passion for dance. Now we're being talked about as role models.'

Ashley Banjo, *Daily Mail* 2009

One of three children to a Nigerian father and an English mother, Ashley experienced prejudice from both black and white communities, and grew up in parts of London that were home to gang culture and knife crime. Ashley's family went through hard times financially — he remembers practising dance moves with the soles falling off his trainers — but he kept working hard, desperately wanting to make a career out of dancing.

In 2007, Ashley and younger brother Jordan formed Swift Moves, the dance troupe that eventually became Diversity. The same year they won a national street dance competition, and in 2009 announced their arrival to the UK public by winning *Britain's Got Talent*.

Diversity continue to perform to packed houses, and Ashley's career — as a dancer, TV presenter and role model — continues to go from strength to strength. All thanks to the power of dance!

Diversity perform one of their eye-popping dance routines at a concert in Cardiff in 2011.

JLS

BOY BAND SENSATION

(From left) JB, Marvin, Oritsé and Aston smile for the cameras in London in 2011.

JLS – standing for 'Jack the Lad Swing' – was the name the guys chose when they entered *The X Factor*, because there was already another group using their original name: UFO.

Stats!

Full names: Aston Iain Merrygold, Marvin Richard James Humes, Oritsé Williams, Jonathan Benjamin 'JB' Gill

Date and place of birth: Aston: 13 February 1988 in Peterborough, UK; Marvin: 18 March 1985 in Greenwich, London, UK; Oritsé: 27 November 1986 in West London, UK; Jonathan: 7 December 1986 in Croydon, London, UK

Education: Poetry was Oritsé's favourite subject at school, which was where he started writing songs.

Big break: The group entered the 2008 series of *The X Factor*, and finished second behind solo singer Alexandra Burke. Their success led to them signing a record contract with Epic Records in January 2009.

Major achievements: JLS's first two albums both sold over one million copies each. They also won 'Best UK Newcomer' and 'Best Song' at the 2009 MOBO Awards, and 'British Breakthrough' and 'British Single' at the 2010 BRIT Awards.

Additional TV appearances: A documentary, *JLS Revealed*, was broadcast on ITV2 in 2009, and the following year *This Is JLS*, which featured the band performing tracks from their second album, was shown on ITV1.

Secrets of success: Hard work and dedication are important to make dance routines and harmonies as good as they can possibly be!

Life Story

Most wannabe pop singers can't wait to get into the music business. But Oritsé Williams actually turned down several offers to be in boy bands because he didn't think the 'chemistry' was right with the other band members. So he took his time, found three friends who shared his ability and dreams and founded UFO (Unique Famous Outrageous) in 2004.

Getting a record deal was difficult, even though the boys won an award for Best Unsigned Act at the 2007 Urban Music Awards, so in 2008 they auditioned for the fifth series of *The X Factor*. They sang and danced their way to the finals, where they finished second, and signed their first proper record deal!

Questions and Answers

Q Are you surprised by how successful you have become?

A 'Sometimes we have to pinch ourselves! [But] we try not to take too much of it in because you don't want to start believing your own hype.'

Jonathan 'JB' Williams, *The Scotsman* 2009

Q Did you worry that coming from a reality show, people would think you were a 'manufactured' band?

A 'If the public felt we weren't authentic they wouldn't have bought our singles. You can't fool people these days… If they didn't think we were credible they wouldn't show us any love.'

Jonathan 'JB' Williams, *The Scotsman* 2009

Six months later, JLS had their first UK Number One with 'Beat Again', and at the start of 2010 the boys signed a US record deal with Jive Records. In November 2011 they released their third album *Jukebox*, which was another huge hit. JLS are the most successful band in the history of *The X Factor* — a little patience from Oritsé has worked wonders!

Michael Sorrentino

JERSEY BOY

Mike's nickname is 'The Situation'. He first used the phrase to describe his own flat six-pack stomach – now the phrase is being sold across the world on T-shirts!

In 2010 Mike was reported to be the highest-earning reality star behind Kim Kardashian, with an estimated income of US$5m (£3.1m).

Stats!

Name: Michael Sorrentino

Date and place of birth: 4 July 1982 in Staten Island, New York, USA

Education: Manalapen High School

Big break: At 25, Mike went to a casting for an unnamed reality TV show that was originally supposed to be shown on VH1. The show was a mess, and producers fired the whole cast apart from Mike. They changed the format and the housemates and named it *Jersey Shore*.

Major achievements: *Jersey Shore* has won record viewing figures for MTV. Thanks to the show' success, Mike has launched a fitness DVD and an autobiography, and is the face of various fitness brands.

Additional TV appearances: Mike appeared on *Dancing With The Stars*, and has been a guest on some of the biggest chat shows in the US, including *The Jay Leno Show* and *The Tonight Show with Conan O'Brien*.

Secrets of success: Mike's catchphrases make him hard to forget. The most famous is GTL: 'gym, tan, laundry' — his favourite daily routine!

Life Story

At 25, Mike Sorrentino was unemployed, single and living at home with his parents. Just four years later he was one of the most famous people in America!

Jersey Shore was first dreamed up as competition — something like *Big Brother*, with housemates voted out over a series of weeks. That was until

Mike (far left) and the rest of the *Jersey Shore* cast arrive at an awards show in Los Angeles in 2010.

new producers decided to make it an antidote to the glamorous lifestyles portrayed in *The Hills*. They collected together eight opinionated New Jersey locals, put them in a beach house for the summer and followed them with cameras 24 hours a day. The show was a huge hit.

Mike has seen his success rise along with *Jersey Shore's* ratings. His diary is filled with nightclub appearances across the US, and he lends his name and image to sports drinks, training shoes and vitamin supplements. There is even talk of Mike and his famous six-pack stomach moving into action movies. It seems that, with Mike, anything is possible!

Cher Lloyd

SINGER WITH THE X FACTOR

Cher's musical style is like her fashion sense — a mixture of modern and classic, sophisticated and fun!

Cher's debut single 'Swagger Jagger' received more than 5 million views on YouTube in less than a month.

Stats!

Name: Cher Lloyd

Date and place of birth: 28 July 1993 in Malvern, Worcestershire, UK.

Big break: Cher had auditioned twice for *The X Factor* and failed to make an impression, but came back for a third year in 2010. Cher's rap/R&B crossover version of Keri Hilson's 'Turn My Swag On' was a big hit with the judges. She made it through to the live shows, finished the series in fourth place, and signed a record deal with Simon Cowell's Syco label.

Major achievements: Cher's first single 'Swagger Jagger' reached Number One on the UK singles chart. The follow-up 'With Ur Love' and Cher's debut album *Sticks & Stones* both reached Number Four in the charts.

Additional TV appearances: Cher made a guest appearance on the 2011 series of *The X Factor*, singing second single 'With Ur Love'.

Secrets of success: Cher has an emotional connection with her fans — she's a typical teenage girl who doesn't mind showing people when she's happy, sad or anywhere in between.

Life Story

Cher Lloyd is probably the only pop star that Malvern has ever produced. From the moment she wowed the *X Factor* audience with her first audition, it was clear the 16 year old from the sleepy West Country town had something special.

Cher had always wanted to perform, and wasn't going to let her isolated location get in the way. She scoured Internet blogs for news on the latest underground music, and taught herself to

Natural born performer: Cher entertains the crowd at the BBC Teen Awards at Wembley Arena in 2011.

rap over instrumentals on YouTube. Now, with a debut Number 1 single and a top-five album, *Sticks & Stones*, to her name, Cher is achieving her full potential.

Growing up as a big personality in a small town, Cher is used to standing up for herself and speaking out for what she believes in. It's been good practice for her musical career, as like all the best pop stars, Cher is like Marmite — love her or hate her, at least you won't forget her!

Questions and Answers

Q **Were you scared of Simon Cowell on the show?**

A 'I was scared to death of Simon sometimes, but in a good way! [He] is nearly always right but I'd still tell him if I didn't agree. If you don't like something then you should just say it... I know Simon respects that.'

Cher Lloyd, *Daily Mirror* 2010

Q **How do you respond to criticism about your music?**

A 'Some people find it hard to come to terms with the fact that everyone is different. I think it all boils down to their own insecurities – if you're unhappy with yourself, you're going to pick on someone else... I feel sorry for them.'

Cher Lloyd, *BLISS* 2011

Paris Hilton

THE REALITY HEIRESS

TV viewers love Paris! Here she launches a new documentary series, 'The World According To Paris', in 2011.

Paris was once refused entry on a flight from Las Vegas to Los Angeles for trying to take a goat, a monkey and a ferret on the plane with her!

Stats!

Name: Paris Whitney Hilton

Date and place of birth: 17 February 1981 in New York City, USA

Education: Paris attended a number of schools in America. In 1999, she was expelled from the Canterbury Boarding School in Connecticut but she later went back to school and earned a GED (General Educational Development) certificate, the equivalent of a high school diploma.

Big break: The Fox TV channel teamed Paris with her good friend Nicole Richie (daughter of singer Lionel) for US reality TV show *The Simple Life*. The show ran for five series, and turned Paris into one of America's first stars of reality TV.

Major achievements: Paris's business empire includes jewellery, cosmetics and clothing. The Paris Hilton name is estimated to generate over US$200m (£125m) per year.

Additional TV appearances: Paris filmed a series for MTV called *Paris Hilton's My New BFF* in 2008, about her search for a 'new best friend'.

Secrets of success: Paris's grandfather Barron Hilton says she works harder than the chairmen of most companies!

Life Story

Paris Hilton's great-grandfather Conrad Hilton created a worldwide chain of top-class hotels. His great-granddaughter has created her own business empire in the Hilton name. Paris was born into a life of privilege, and spent her teenage years travelling the US with her family, appearing on red carpets and attending VIP events with friends including Kimberley Stewart (daughter of singer Rod), and actresses Lindsay Lohan and Tara Reid.

Fun-loving Paris also knew how to grab opportunities when they came along. The reality show *A Simple Life* was her launching pad to a multi-million dollar business empire that stretches from TV to property development to designer handbags. Paris has appeared in several Hollywood movies (she won a Teen Choice Award for 'Best Scream'

TV success has given Paris the opportunity to branch out, such as launching her own range of denim and sportswear.

Questions and Answers

Q Did growing up rich make it easier for you to achieve your goals?

A 'A lot of my friends still live at home and have to ask their parents for everything. I haven't accepted money from my parents since I was 18. Since then, I've worked on my own. It feels good that I don't have to depend on [them].'

Paris Hilton, *The Guardian* 2008

Q What's the secret of your success?

A 'I'm a businesswoman... and I love to work. I think it just runs through my veins. My great-grandfather [Conrad Hilton] was a bellboy and had a dream to build a hotel chain, so I think I get it from him.'

Paris Hilton, *The Guardian* 2008

for the 2005 horror film *House of Wax*), and written a *New York Times* best-selling autobiography *Confessions Of An Heiress*. She even released an album, *Paris*, in 2006, and the first single 'Stars Are Blind' was Number One in 17 countries!

These days Paris seems happy to spend less time in front of the camera, and more time taking care of business. Perhaps she could be the next Alan Sugar?

Peter Andre

TV's MR NICE GUY

Peter takes fatherhood very seriously, and has been voted Dad of the Year twice!

Peter is scared of spiders – it's the only phobia he didn't overcome in the 'I'm A Celebrity...' jungle!

Stats!

Name: Peter James Andrea

Date and place of birth: 27 February 1973 in London, England

Education: Peter attended Sudbury Junior School in London, and Benowa High School in Queensland after his parents emigrated to Australia.

Big break: At 16, Peter won an Australian TV talent contest, and launched his singing career. But it was his appearance in the 2004 series of ITV1's *I'm A Celebrity... Get Me Out Of Here!* and his romance with model Katie Price that launched Peter's second career as a reality TV star.

Major achievements: As a singer, Peter has topped the UK singles charts, and sold out London's O2 arena. As a TV star, his shows are ratings winners for ITV2. In fact, his show *The Next Chapter* got double the ratings of Katie Price's new series, when the pair split up.

Additional TV appearances: Out of the jungle, *Pete and Katie* launched their own fly-on-the-wall reality show *Katie & Peter* that ran for four years. After the pair separated, Peter made three solo reality shows, *Peter Andre: Going It Alone*, *Peter Andre: The Next Chapter* and *Peter Andre: Here to Help*.

Secrets of success: Peter presents himself as a genuinely likable character who is a natural in front of the camera. He aims to make even the school run interesting viewing!

Life Story

At 13, Peter Andre wrote his first song. At 16, he entered a TV talent contest in Australia, and was so impressive he was offered a record contract live on air. He moved to the UK in 1992 and had two Number One singles and a platinum-selling album. But by 1998 the hits were running out and Peter returned to Australia to help his parents run the family beach

Questions and Answers

Q 'Was *I'm A Celebrity...* a life-changing event for you?

A 'Definitely. Life changing in many ways. Career-wise – definitely. Relationship-wise – definitely. And I conquered my fears [of snakes and heights]. You go to therapy for years to overcome some of your fears, and I did it in two weeks!'

Peter Andre, *www.virginactive.com* 2010

Q Do you enjoy watching yourself on TV?

A '[Argh, no!] There are so many times you watch yourself and think, 'Why did I say that?' [But] I can't regret it – it's my job, and there will always be bits of your job you don't like.'

Peter Andre, *The Guardian* 2009

resort. Even his fans thought his headlining days were behind him.

However, in 2004 Peter was invited to take part in ITV1's jungle hit *I'm A Celebrity...* On the show he met, and fell in love with, model Katie Price and, just as importantly, the British public fell back in love with Peter! A rerelease of one of his earliest singles 'Mysterious Girl' went to Number One, and the couple's reality show *Katie & Peter* became a success.

The cameras followed the pair through their daily lives — in the kitchen, on the school run, at the gym — and as ordinary as it sounds, the show was watched by millions. When Katie and Peter divorced, they both launched solo shows, and Peter continues to live his life in front of an audience. He was born to entertain.

Peter and his then wife Katie Price ran side by side in the 2009 London Marathon to raise money for the NSPCC.

17

Audrina Patridge

Audrina moved to Los Angeles to be an actress, but found fame as a reality star.

Audrina owns a US$5,000 (£3,148) Chanel surfboard – but has never used it for surfing!

Stats!

Full name: Audrina Cathleen Patridge

Date and place of birth: 9 May 1985 in Placentia, California, USA

Education: Audrina graduated from El Dorado High School in Placentia, Orange County, and started studying child psychology before dropping out to move to Los Angeles and pursue a career as an actress.

Big break: Producers for a new reality show *The Hills* visited Audrina's apartment building in LA looking for places to shoot. They spotted her sunbathing by the pool and interviewed her for the show. She started filming three weeks later, and ended up appearing in all six series.

Major achievements: As one of *The Hills*' four original cast members, Audrina played a vital role in the show's success. She appeared in more episodes than any other cast member, and has become a household name in the US.

Additional TV appearances: Audrina has featured in *Dancing With The Stars*, the US equivalent of *Strictly Come Dancing*. She also starred in her own reality series, *Audrina*.

Secrets of success: Audrina's sense of style has been a big hit with the US public. During the show, she worked with lots of US fashion labels, and even has a jumper named after her!

Life Story

It's a dream for lots of teenagers to move to Los Angeles and become famous. For Audrina Patridge, it happened while she was lying on a sunbed!

Relocating to LA from her home in Orange County, Audrina found a part-time job as a receptionist and was taking acting classes when circumstances brought her face to face with *The Hills* production crew who visited the apartment building she was living in.

Questions and Answers

Q **What was the worst thing about appearing in *The Hills*?**

A 'Everyone has an opinion [about you] even though they don't know the truth... I used to read everything that people said about me, but then I realised that if you care about what everyone else thinks and try to please them all, you'll end up [driving yourself crazy!]

Audrina Patridge, *FHM* 2011

Q **What's your plan for life after the show?**

A 'I want to make people laugh! I think it would be fun to do a comedy or romantic comedy film. I am going to [loads of] auditions now for TV and film projects.'

Audrina Patridge, *Bayfront magazine* 2010

Audrina was hired as the 'best friend' of stars Heidi Montag, and Lauren Conrad, who was filming a spin-off series to the hit *Laguna Beach: The Real Orange County*. Both shows are examples of a recent TV phenomenon called 'scripted reality' where real people 'act' certain situations that are set up or suggested by producers — from going shopping, to arguing with a boyfriend.

The Hills was a huge success for MTV, and turned the cast into stars. Audrina has appeared on magazine covers around the world, and was given her own reality show, *Audrina*, when *The Hills* ended after six series. Her (reality) star keeps on rising.

Audrina and her dance partner Tony Dovolani at the launch of 'Dancing With The Stars' in 2010.

Jordin Sparks

AMERICAN IDOL

Jordin has sold over 9 million singles, making her one of the most successful American Idol winners.

When she turned 18, Jordin, her mum and grandmother all had their favourite Bible verses tattooed on the inside of their wrists!

Stats!

Full name: Jordin Brianna Sparks

Date and place of birth: 22 December 1989 in Phoenix, Arizona, USA

Education: Jordin attended Sandra Day O'Connor High School in Phoenix until 2006, and then was taught at home so she could spend more time on her singing.

Big break: In summer 2006 Jordin attended *American Idol* auditions in Los Angeles but failed to progress. She then won a local talent contest 'Arizona Idol', and was encouraged to audition for *American Idol* again — this time in Seattle. She impressed the judges and went on to win the series!

Major achievements: Jordin's debut album *Jordin Sparks* sold over 2 million copies, and she is the first *American Idol* winner to reach the top 20 on the American Billboard Hot 100 chart with her first five singles. She has sold over 9 million singles worldwide.

Additional TV appearances: Jordin has returned several times to perform new songs on *American Idol*. She has also made a guest appearance on US TV shows *The Suite Life On Deck*, *Big Time Rush* and *When I Was 17*.

Secrets of success: Jordin's voice, talent and personality have made her one of America's favourite TV personalities.

Life Story

When Jordin Sparks became *American Idol's* youngest ever winner in 2007, a massive 74 million votes were cast. Reality talent contests create huge potential audiences for the contestants. But not every winner has the long-running success that Jordin has enjoyed.

Since her victory, she has achieved million-selling albums and singles, sung the national anthem at the Super Bowl, and performed in award-winning Broadway musical *In The Heights*.

Questions and Answers

Q How did it feel to win *American Idol*?

A 'I've been watching the show [since it started] and I always told my mum every year during the final show, 'I want to be able to sing on that stage. Whether I win or not, I want to be there!' To actually do it [was amazing].'

Jordin Sparks, *American Idol blog* 2010

Q Do you still watch the show?

A 'I do! I was a fan before I was on it and I've continued to watch it since. When [I see] the new contestants, I say to myself 'I know what you're going through right now. Don't worry.' It's amazing that [the show] gives all these people a chance to do amazing things.'

Jordin Sparks, *AOL Music blog* 2011

Like other reality TV stars, Jordin has been able to use her popularity to expand into new areas of interest. She launched her own fragrance 'Because Of You...' in 2010, and is a spokesperson for Avon's teenage cosmetics.

Jordin also uses her popularity to help people less fortunate than herself. She travelled to Ghana to help raise awareness of the dangers of malaria, and has performed at fund-raising events for children's hospitals and environmental awareness.

Jordin sings the National Anthem at the US Super Bowl in 2008. The event was watched by a billion people around the world!

OTHER REALITY TV STARS

Olly Murs

Education: Olly attended Howbridge Junior School in Witham, then Notley High School in Braintree, Essex.

Background: Olly played as a semi-professional footballer, but had to give up the sport because of injury. He moved from job to job, working as a fitness instructor, and in a call centre selling kitchens.

Big break: Olly entered *The X Factor* in 2007 and 2008 but never made it through the auditions. In 2009, he entered for a third time and went all the way to the final where he finished second.

Career highs: Olly's debut single 'Please Don't Let Me Go' went to Number One in August 2010, and his debut album sold over 600,000 copies. His second album In Case You Didn't Know was released in November 2011.

Fast fact: Olly was forced to miss his twin brother's wedding because it was scheduled for the same day as *The X Factor* semi-finals and Simon Cowell wouldn't let him leave the rehearsal studio!

Website: www.ollymurs.com

Basic Information

Home: Born and still lives in Witham, Essex.

Born: 14 May 1984

Mark Wright

Education: Mark was a student at the famous Sylvia Young talent school in London, but left at 16 to join Tottenham Hotspur FC as a trainee.

Background: Released at 18 by Tottenham Hotspur, Mark continued to play semi-professional football while working as a club promoter in his native Essex.

Big break: ITV bosses working on a new 'scripted reality' series *The Only Way Is Essex* (TOWIE) cast Mark and his then fiancée Lauren Goodger as two of the main characters.

Career highs: After winning a BAFTA award with his TOWIE co-stars in 2011, Mark left the show after three series, and has since appeared in *I'm A Celebrity... Get Me Out Of Here!*

Fast fact: Mark's younger brother Josh is a professional footballer who plays for Millwall FC

Website: www.markwrightofficial.co.uk

Basic Information

Home: Born and still lives in Buckhurst Hill, Essex.

Born: 20 January 1987

Lauren Conrad

Education: Lauren attended Laguna Beach High School in her home town.

Background: As one of the stars of MTV's first reality series *Laguna Beach: The Real Orange County*, Lauren combined her love of fashion with a heavy filming schedule. She attended the Academy of Art University in San Francisco for one term, and then returned to Laguna Beach to study design and marketing.

Big break: Laguna Beach's success led to a spin-off series, *The Hills*, which followed the lives of Lauren and her friends (including Audrina Patridge and Heidi Montag) in Los Angeles. Lauren starred in the show from January 2007 until May 2009.

Career highs: After appearing in five series of *The Hills*, Lauren left the show. She has since written a series of books for young adults, *LA Candy Trilogy*, which is being made into a film, and has featured as a guest judge on *America's Next Top Model*.

Fast fact: Lauren was rumoured to be earning US$75,000 (£47,000) per episode for *The Hills*.

Website: www.laurenconrad.com

Basic Information

Home: Born in Laguna Beach, California, USA. Lives in Los Angeles, California, USA.

Born: 1 February 1986

Kourtney Kardashian

Basic Information

Home: Born in Mill Valley, California, USA. Lives in Los Angeles, California, USA.

Born: 18 April 1979

Education: Like her younger sister Kim, Kourtney went to the prestigious all-girls Marymount High School in Beverly Hills. She then attended Southern Methodist University in Dallas, Texas, and the University of Arizona, graduating with a degree in theatre arts and Spanish.

Background: Kourtney is the daughter of famous LA lawyer Robert Kardashian who was one of OJ Simpson's defence team during his murder trial in 1995.

Big break: Kourtney's family became reality TV stars in the hit series *Keeping Up With The Kardashians*.

Career highs: Kourtney has starred in spin-off series *Kourtney and Khloé Take Miami*, and *Kourtney And Kim Take New York*.

Fast fact: Kourtney's first TV appearance was on a series called *Filthy Rich: Cattle Drive* in 2005, where the children of rich and famous parents worked on a cattle ranch to raise money for charity.

Website: http://officialkourtneyk.celebuzz.com/

Tamara Ecclestone

Basic Information

Home: Born in Milan, Italy. Lives in London, England.

Born: 28 June 1984

Education: Tamara went to the private Francis Holland School in Notting Hill, London and earned 4 A* grades at A-level.

Background: Tamara is the daughter of the multi-billionaire boss of Formula One, Bernie Ecclestone. After finishing school, she went to the London School of Economics, and then University College London, but did not complete her degree. She now runs her own business producing a range of hair care products.

Big break: Tamara's millionaire lifestyle was the subject of the three-part reality series *Tamara Ecclestone: Billion Dollar Girl*, which was shown on Channel Five in November 2011.

Career highs: Tamara presented Formula One coverage on Sky Sports Italia for two years – in Italian! She also presented the Red Bull Air Race for Channel 4.

Fast fact: In 2011, Tamara's dad Bernie was ranked as the fourth richest man in Britain.

Website: www.tamaraecclestone.com

Paul DelVecchio

Basic Information

Home: Born and still lives in Providence, Rhode Island USA.

Born: 5 July 1980

Education: Paul, usually known by his nickname Pauly D, attended Johnston High School in Rhode Island.

Background: Pauly started out as a local club DJ, hosting his own parties and dreaming of making it big.

Big break: *Jersey Shore* producers sent Pauly D a message through social networking site MySpace. They sent a film crew from LA to Rhode Island to film his everyday life – gym, tanning salon, nightclub – and six months later asked him to be one of the show's founder members!

Career highs: Pauly D is the show's funnyman, and music lover. In 2011 he won the Teen Choice Award for Male Reality Star, and announced a three-album deal with rapper 50 Cent's G-Unit Records.

Fast fact: Pauly D was Britney Spears' DJ for her Femme Fatale tour, and performed for Kim Kardashian at the opening of her DASH clothing store in New York City.

Website: http://www.djpaulyd.com/main/

More reality TV stars to look out for

Khloé Kardashian — *Khloé & Lamar, Kourtney And Khloé Take Miami*

Hilary Devey — *Secret Millionaire, Dragons' Den*

Heidi Montag — *The Hills*

John and Edward Grimes (aka Jedward) — *The X Factor, Celebrity Big Brother*

Amy Childs — *The Only Way Is Essex, All About Amy*

Index